MW01703474

A daily journal designed to improve physical, emotional, and spiritual well-being.

GoodStandard

“I can do nothing for you
but work on myself…
you can do nothing for me
but work on yourself!”

— **Ram Dass**

WELCOME TO THE UNF*@K YOUR ENERGY JOURNAL

You're about to embark on a transformative journey to reclaim the most authentic, powerful version of yourself. The Unf*@k Your Energy Journal is designed to be different, effective, and life-changing because it merges ancient wisdom with modern science in a practical, actionable format. This journal isn't just a collection of prompts; it's a carefully curated guide to help you explore and heal the deepest parts of your psyche, emotions, and energy.

TABLE OF CONTENTS

INTRODUCTION

As a Clinical Psychologist, I am always seeking tools that support personal growth and emotional well-being. This journal is designed to facilitate self-reflection and mindfulness, offering prompts that encourage introspection and emotional exploration. It can be used on its own or in conjunction with psychotherapy to process anything that arises during this journey.

When you are ready to begin, I recommend creating a peaceful space for contemplation. Settle into a comfortable position, and start with a few slow, deep breaths–placing one hand on your belly and the other on your heart, breathing in through the nose if possible, and allowing the belly to rise and fall. After a few cycles, read a prompt and let it guide your thoughts.

Pay attention to sensations in the body, and if any memories or images surface, take a moment to reflect on them. Keep your journal nearby to capture your insights. Pages are left intentionally blank so that you can draw as well as write what comes to mind.

Remember to treat yourself with care and patience throughout this process. Incorporate gentle activities like stretching, gentle exercise, walks and/or connecting with nature to support your journey. Drink plenty of water, maintain a healthy diet, and allow yourself time to rest. Your body and mind are working together to heal, and it's essential to nurture yourself along the way.

It's important to note that some of these exercises may bring up thoughts and feelings that may be uncomfortable. If, at any point, you feel overwhelmed, or if your daily life, relationships, or work are affected, please reach out to a mental health professional or a crisis line for support.

By Dr. Erica Felsenthal,
Ph.D. Clinical Neuropsychologist,
Good Standard Advisory Board

Disclaimer

This is not psychotherapy. This program is only for informational and educational purposes and should not be considered therapy or any form of treatment. Please check with your doctor to make sure these suggestions are appropriate for you. If you are having difficulty with your normal routines or having any thoughts of harming yourself or someone else, please seek professional mental health support immediately. We are not able to respond to specific questions or comments about personal situations, appropriate diagnosis or treatment, or otherwise provide any clinical opinions in this program. If you think you need immediate assistance, call your local emergency number or the mental health crisis hotline listed in your local community's mental health resources or government pages.

The Methodology:

Going Deep: When engaging with each prompt, take your time. Allow yourself to dig beneath the surface and explore the underlying emotions, beliefs, and memories that come up. The goal is to unpack these layers and bring what is hidden into the light of awareness.

Freewriting: This is a powerful tool for accessing your subconscious mind. As you respond to each prompt, write freely without censoring yourself. Let your thoughts flow without worrying about grammar, spelling, or structure. This process can help you tap into deeper insights and emotions.

Making the Unseen Seen: Carl Jung famously said, "Until you make the unconscious conscious, it will direct your life and you will call it fate." The prompts in this journal are designed to do exactly that–make the unconscious conscious. By bringing hidden thoughts, emotions, and patterns to the surface, you gain the power to change them.

How This Works:

Integration of Concepts: The prompts integrate concepts from shadow work, inner child healing, energy alignment, and neuroscience. This holistic approach aims to help you find the root causes of your challenges, not just the symptoms.

Self-Awareness: By engaging with these prompts, you will likely increase your self-awareness. You may begin to notice patterns in your thoughts, behaviors, and emotions, allowing you to make conscious choices rather than being driven by unconscious impulses.

Healing and Growth: The ultimate goal of this work is healing and personal growth. As you confront and process old wounds, limiting beliefs, and unhelpful patterns, you may feel a sense of increased space for new, healthier ways of being.

Potential Benefits of Doing This Work:

Emotional Clarity: You may gain clarity around your emotions, understanding where they come from and how to process them in a healthy way.

Increased Confidence: By working through the blocks in your Solar Plexus energy center, you may feel improved self-confidence and a stronger sense of personal power.

Deeper Relationships: As you open up your Heart energy center, you might find it easier to connect with others, give and receive love, and cultivate compassion.

Greater Stability: Strengthening your Root energy center might result in feeling more grounded, secure, and capable of handling life's challenges.

Creative Flow: Tapping into your Sacral energy center could help you feel like you've unleashed your creativity and may help you express your emotions in a healthy way.

How to Use the Prompts

You can approach the prompts in two ways:

Follow the Sequence: The prompts are organized to start with the Root energy center and move upwards through the Sacral, Solar Plexus, Heart, and so on. This order helps you build a strong foundation before moving into higher levels of consciousness and self-expression.

Choose Your Focus: If you feel drawn to a particular area, such as relationships or creativity, you can jump to the relevant section and work on those prompts. The journal is designed to be flexible to meet your needs.

Understanding the Components

This journal blends powerful practices like shadow work, inner child healing, energy healing (through the chakra system), and insights from modern neuroscience. Each of these components offers a different lens to examine, understand, and heal the deeper layers of your psyche. By addressing trauma, beliefs, and patterns stored in the body and mind, this journal guides you to uncover and release what no longer serves you.

The prompts are designed to be simple yet profound, encouraging you to explore your inner world, make the unconscious conscious, and transform your life from the inside out. Whether you're working on emotional healing, personal growth, or spiritual development, these practices are here to help you build stronger foundations and step into your most authentic self.

Shadow Work

Shadow work is the process of uncovering and integrating the parts of ourselves that we've repressed or denied–our "shadow." These can include feelings of anger, shame, guilt, or other aspects we find uncomfortable. Popularized by Carl Jung, shadow work is rooted in Jungian psychology. Jung believed that the shadow is a necessary part of our psyche, and integrating it is crucial for personal growth. By confronting these hidden parts, we gain a fuller understanding of ourselves, which can lead to greater self-acceptance, better relationships, and more control over our lives

Inner Child Work

Inner child work involves connecting with and healing the part of ourselves that still holds onto the traumas, fears, and unmet needs from our childhood. Stemming from various psychological practices, inner child work has been used to address deep-seated emotional issues by acknowledging and nurturing our childlike aspects. When we heal our inner child, we break free from limiting beliefs and patterns that were formed in early life, allowing us to lead a more fulfilled and authentic life.

Energy Healing/Chakra Work

Energy healing focuses on balancing the body's energy centers (Chakras) to promote physical, emotional, and spiritual well-being. Originating in ancient Indian spiritual traditions, Chakra work involves the alignment of seven primary energy centers in the body, each corresponding to different aspects of our lives. Aligning these energy centers can release stored trauma, improve mental clarity, and enhance overall vitality.

Neuroscience

Neuroscience is the study of the brain and nervous system, focusing on how our brains influence our behaviors, emotions, and overall mental health. Modern neuroscience supports the benefits of mindfulness, meditation, and self-reflection–practices that are core to shadow work, inner child healing, and energy work. Understanding how our brain works empowers us to rewire it, leading to healthier thought patterns and behaviors.

The Unf*@k Your Energy Pledge :

By opening this journal, I commit to showing up for myself fully and unapologetically. I pledge to explore, express, and embrace every part of my being, even the parts I've hidden away. This is my space to get real, get messy, and get weird–without fear, without judgment.

I set my intention to:

- Use these pages to unburden my heart, free my mind, and explore my truth.
- Create without limits–whether that means writing, drawing, tearing, or building something new.
- Be patient and gentle with myself as I dive deep into my emotions, fears, and dreams.
- Trust that everything I uncover will bring me closer to my most authentic, unf*@ked self.
- Let this journal be my companion on the path to growth, healing, and freedom.
- I am ready. I am worthy. I am powerful.

Let's do this thing:

Signature: ______________________________

Date: __________________________________

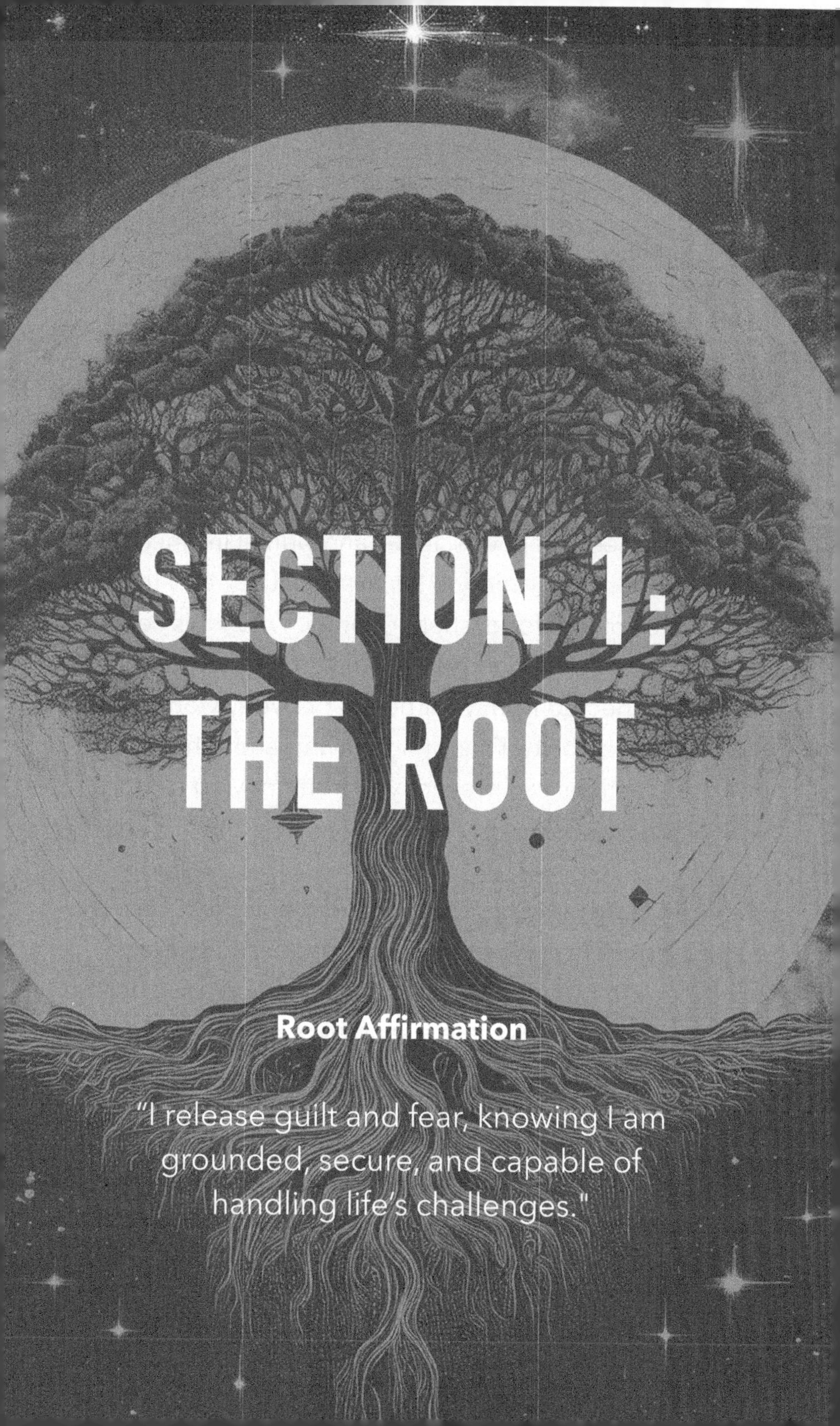

SECTION 1: THE ROOT

Root Affirmation

"I release guilt and fear, knowing I am grounded, secure, and capable of handling life's challenges."

Section 1: The Root

Focus: Stability, Security, Survival

The Root Energy Center is all about our foundation. It's where our deepest needs, fears, and primal instincts lie. This center is closely tied to survival, security, and the basic necessities of life—food, shelter, safety. When this center is out of balance, fear and guilt often surface, and you might feel disconnected from your needs or overly worried about survival and stability. Fear of not having enough or guilt over past actions can prevent you from moving forward with a strong, secure foundation.

<u>Work in this section:</u> Explore and release fear-based beliefs, confront survival anxieties, and examine areas where you may feel guilty for prioritizing your own needs. This work helps you create a sense of safety within yourself, allowing you to address your most basic human needs with confidence and self-compassion.

What does safety mean to you?
How do you create a sense of safety in your life?

Reflect on a time when you felt insecure or unsafe.
How did you overcome it?

What fears hold you back from feeling fully grounded?
How can you address them?

How does your financial situation affect your sense of security?

Describe a place where you feel most grounded and secure. Get detailed.

What daily practices help you stay connected to your body and the present moment?

Reflect on a time when you felt guilty for something beyond your control. How can you release this unnecessary guilt and find peace in accepting the past?

Reflect on your relationship with
your home environment.
How could it better support you?

What are your core beliefs about money and stability?
Where do these beliefs come from?

Identify a past trauma that impacts your sense of security.
What steps can you take to start healing it?

Identify one recurring situation where guilt holds you back. What steps can you take to transform this guilt into constructive action?

What role does your physical health play in your overall sense of well-being?

What would it feel like to forgive yourself fully? Visualize the freedom of moving forward without guilt weighing you down.

How do you navigate changes and transitions in your life?

What practical steps can you take to
strengthen your foundation in life?

SECTION 2: THE SACRAL

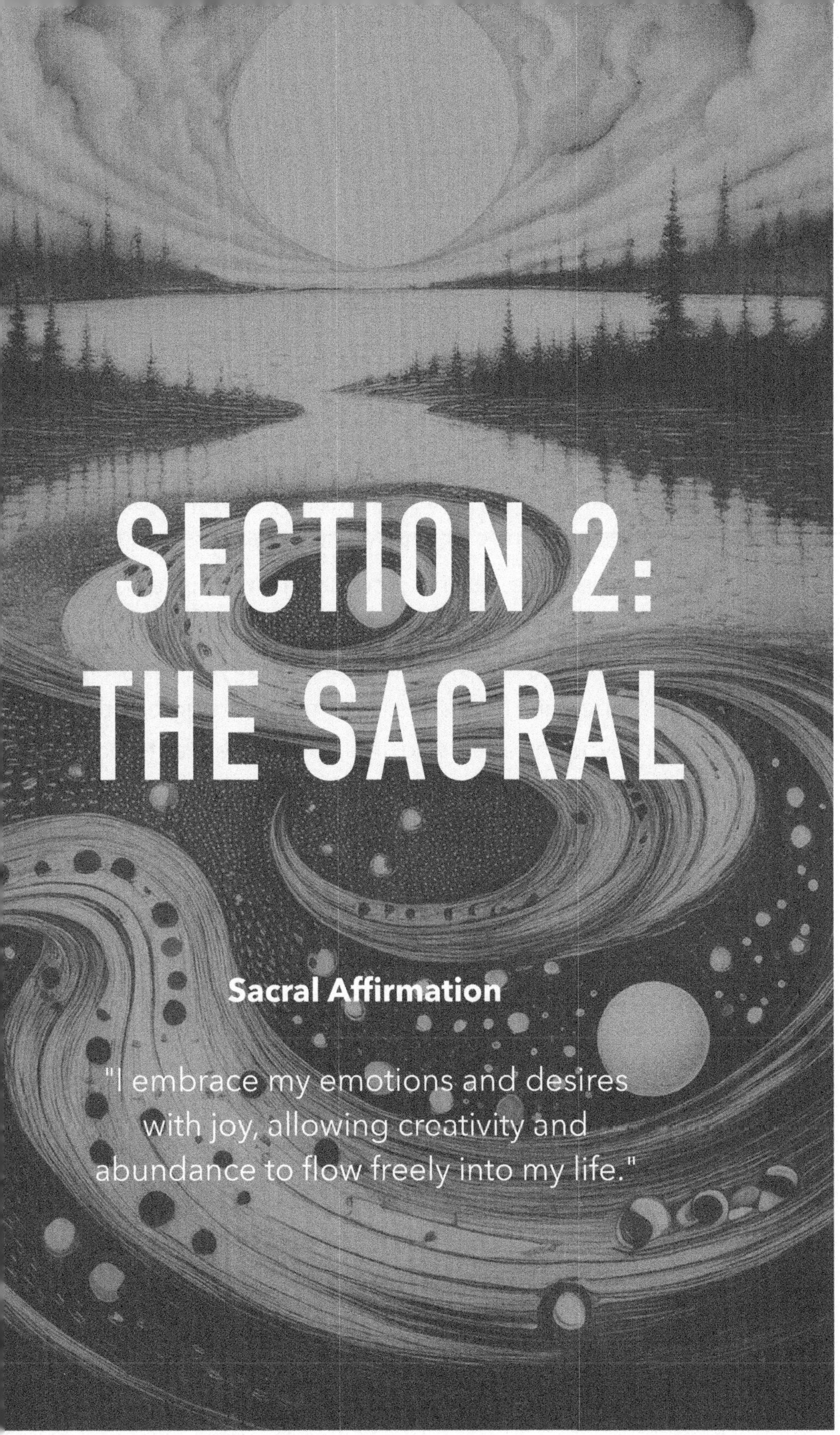

Sacral Affirmation

"I embrace my emotions and desires with joy, allowing creativity and abundance to flow freely into my life."

Section 2: The Sacral

Focus: Creativity, Sexuality, Emotional Expression

The Sacral Energy Center is where your emotions, creativity, and sense of worth live. It's deeply connected to feelings of pleasure, abundance, and how you set boundaries with others. When this center is blocked, feelings of shame, scarcity, or a belief that you can only have "just enough" may arise. You might struggle with expressing your needs or desires, or feel hesitant about setting boundaries out of fear of rejection.

Work in this section: Examine areas where you feel shame, a lack of worth, or struggle with setting healthy boundaries. Release the idea that you are only allowed "just enough" and begin to open yourself to the possibility of abundance, joy, and emotional balance. Recognize where you may be holding yourself back from fully feeling or expressing your desires and begin reclaiming your sense of worth.

What creative activities bring you the most joy?
How can you incorporate them more into your life?

Reflect on your relationship with your sexuality.
How do you express this aspect of yourself?

What emotions do you find difficult to express? Why?

Describe a time when you felt creatively blocked.
What helped you break through it?

Think about a moment when shame kept you from expressing your true self. How can you embrace vulnerability to move past this?

Reflect on your current relationships. Do these relationships provide you with a sense of emotional satisfaction and support?

What role does pleasure play in your life?
Do you allow yourself to experience and
embrace it fully, and how?

How do you express your emotions?
Is there a healthier way you can do this?

What is your relationship with your body?
How do you care for it?

Identify a past experience that shaped your views on creativity or sexuality. How has it impacted you?

How do you balance logic and emotion
in your daily decisions?

Reflect on a time when you felt deeply connected to someone. What made it so?

How can acknowledging your imperfections be a pathway to deeper self-acceptance?

What inspires you? How can you bring more of that inspiration into your daily life?

Write about a desire you have that you've never acted on. What's holding you back?

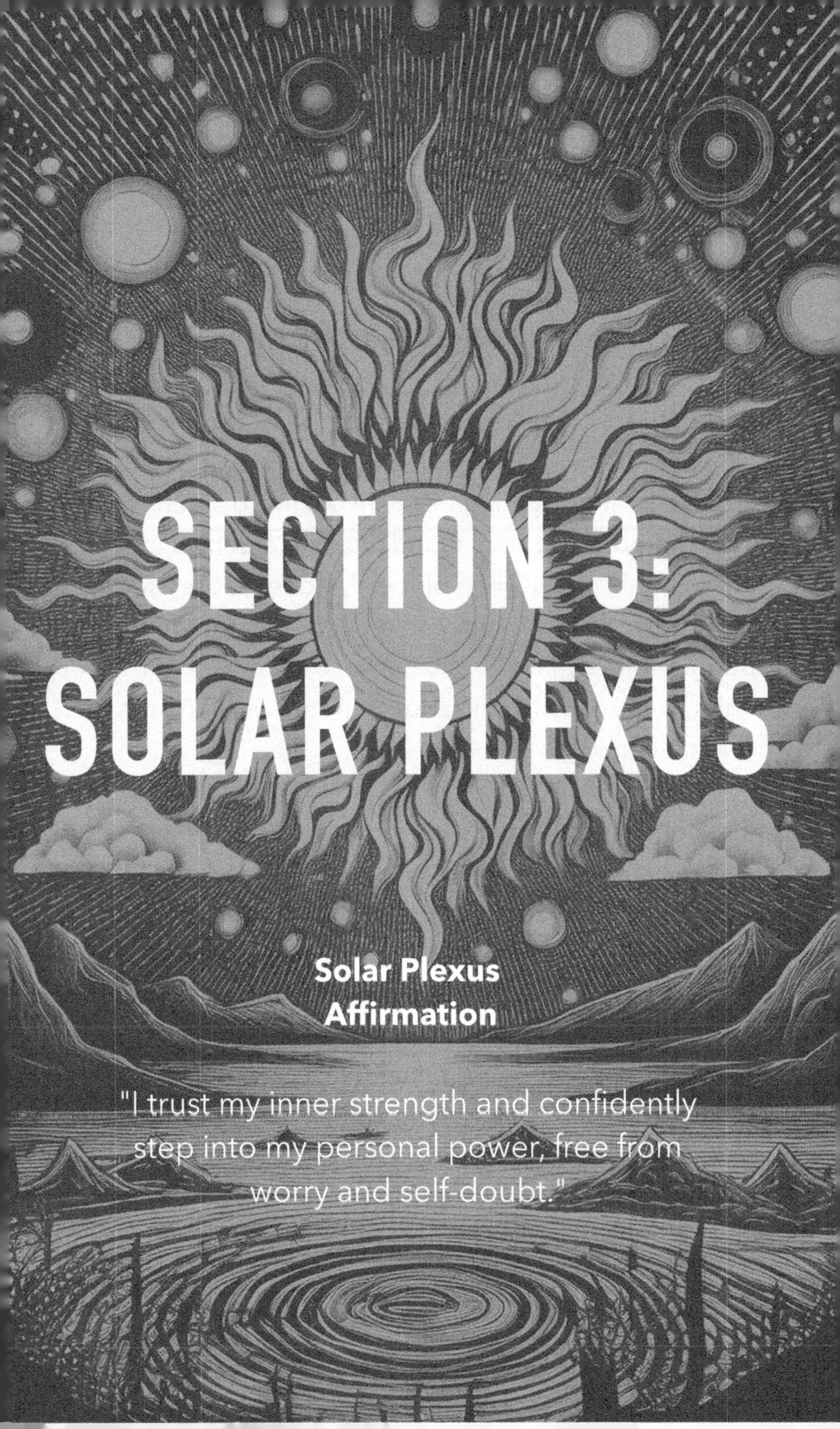

SECTION 3: SOLAR PLEXUS

Solar Plexus Affirmation

"I trust my inner strength and confidently step into my personal power, free from worry and self-doubt."

Section 3: The Solar Plexus

Focus: Personal Power, Confidence, Identity

The Solar Plexus Energy Center is where your identity, self-worth, and inner power reside. It's the seat of your personal strength, confidence, and ability to assert yourself. A sturdy Root and Sacral foundation are essential for this center to thrive, but when blocked, it often looks like worry, fear, chronic self-sabotage, or low self-esteem. You may struggle with feelings of shame, have difficulty setting healthy boundaries, or find yourself stuck in worst-case-scenario thinking.

<u>Work in this section:</u> Uncover where your confidence has been shaken or compromised. Explore moments where worry, fear, or shame has caused you to shrink away from your personal power or avoid expressing your true self. Look for patterns of self-sabotage and ask where they stem from. This work helps you to rebuild your self-esteem and redefine your identity on your terms, one that is free from old fear-based patterns and shame. Through this, you reclaim your sense of worth and step into your authentic self.

What does personal power mean to you?
How do you claim it in your life?

Reflect on a time when you felt
confident and empowered.
What contributed to that feeling?

How do you handle situations where
your boundaries are tested?

Write about your core values.
How do they shape your decisions and actions?

What is your relationship with self-doubt?
How can you combat it?

Reflect on the worries that constantly occupy your mind. How would your life change if you allowed yourself to trust your inner strength?

How do you assert yourself in your relationships and work?

Write about a time when worry kept you from pursuing something you desired. How can you shift from worry to confidence in similar situations going forward?

Identify a past experience that undermined your confidence. How can you heal from it?

How do you respond to criticism?
Is there a healthier way to process it?

Reflect on your personal goals.
How do they align with your sense of identity?

What role does fear play in your life?
How can you confront it?

How do you celebrate your achievements?
Is there room for more self-recognition?

Write about a decision you made confidently.
What did you learn from it?

How do you maintain your sense of self in the face of external pressures?

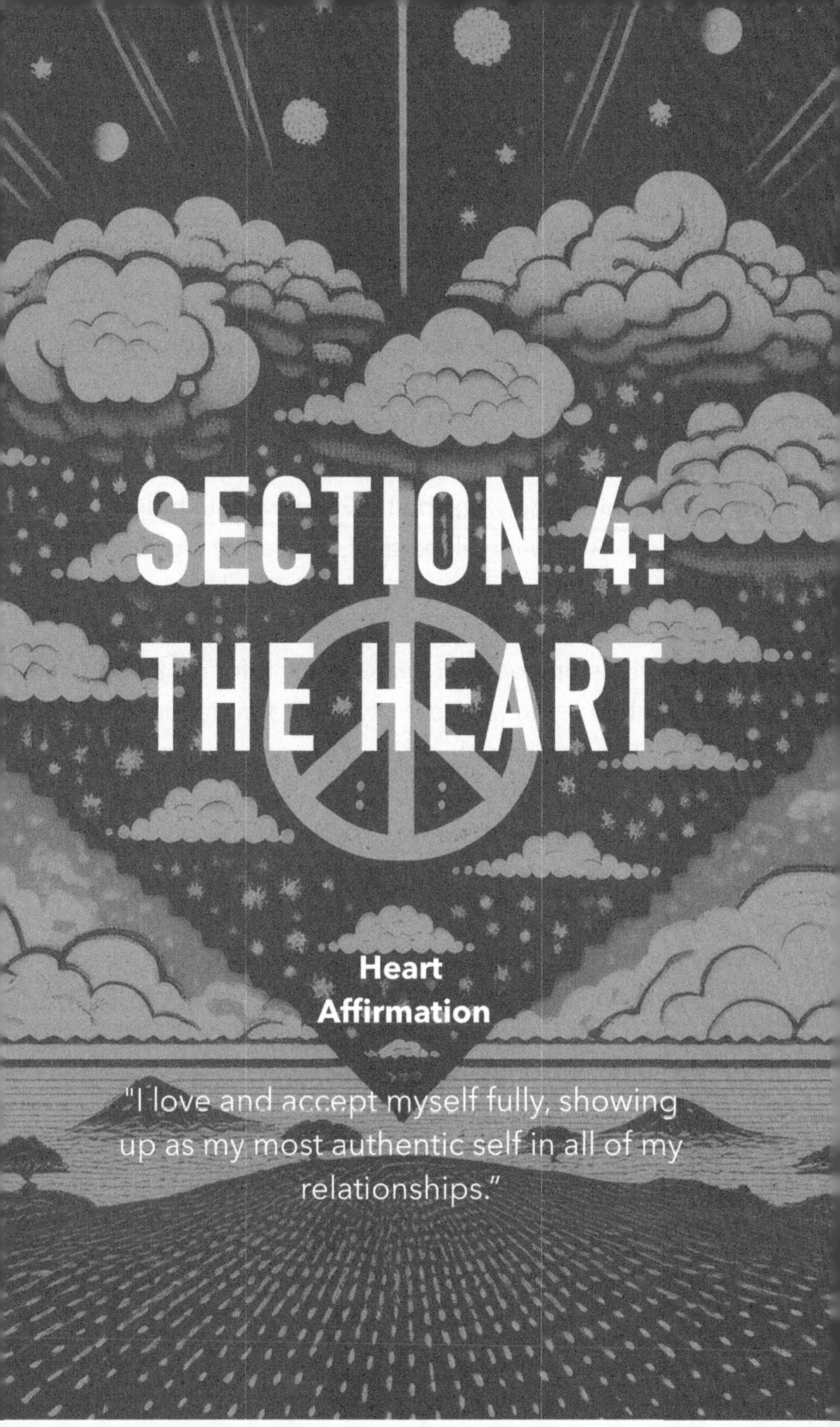

SECTION 4: THE HEART

Heart Affirmation

"I love and accept myself fully, showing up as my most authentic self in all of my relationships."

Section 4: The Heart

Focus: Authenticity, Love, Compassion, Connection

The heart is where the journey to authenticity begins. This energy center is about love–for yourself and others. It's about embracing who you truly are, without hiding or pretending. Accepting all parts of yourself–the good, the flawed, the scared, and the loving–without shame.

Here, you stop needing masks or walls for protection. As you embrace your authenticity, you form deeper, more genuine connections with others. The real you is enough. Accepting yourself naturally leads to accepting others, creating a life filled with honest, meaningful relationships.

<u>Work in this section:</u> Uncover the beliefs and experiences that block you from self-love. Explore self-compassion and embrace vulnerability as a strength. Let go of the need to hide and build confidence in showing your true self. Reflect on how accepting yourself allows you to form deeper connections with others. Practice forgiving yourself and others to open space for unconditional love. The heart is where you find the courage to be you, unapologetically.

What does love mean to you?
How do you express it to yourself and others?

Reflect on a time when you felt truly loved.

What past hurts are you holding onto?
How can you begin to release them?

How do you practice self-love?
Is there room for improvement?

Write about a time when you
forgave someone. How did it feel?

Reflect on your relationships. Are they balanced in terms of giving and receiving?

How do you handle feelings of jealousy or envy?
What triggers these emotions?

Write about someone who inspires you with their compassion. What can you learn from them?

How do you show compassion to
yourself in difficult times?

Reflect on a time when you felt deeply connected to someone. What contributed to that strong sense of connection?

How do you practice empathy in your daily life?

What does forgiveness mean to you?
How do you practice it?

Reflect on a relationship where you've withheld your true feelings. What would authentic communication look like in that situation?

When have you struggled to show up as your most authentic self? What external factors influence this, and how can you overcome them?

Reflect on your relationship with your family.
How can you heal any rifts or strengthen your bond?

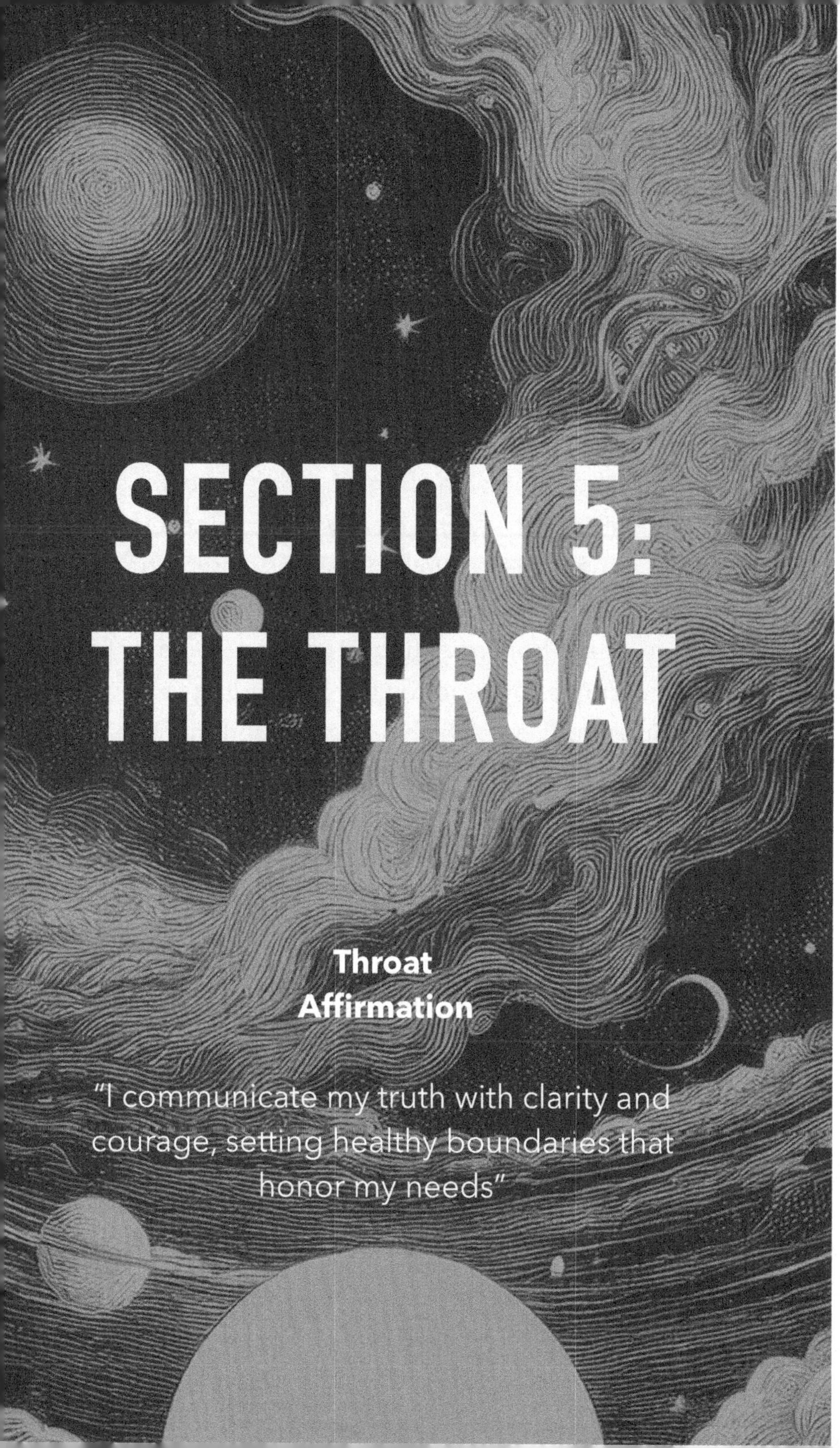

SECTION 5: THE THROAT

Throat Affirmation

"I communicate my truth with clarity and courage, setting healthy boundaries that honor my needs"

Section 5: The Throat

Focus: Communication, Self-Expression, Truth

The Throat Energy Center governs your communication, both with others and with yourself. It's about expressing your truth authentically and clearly. When blocked, it may manifest as negative self-talk, gossip, spreading rumors, or other toxic speaking behaviors like passive-aggressiveness or holding back from speaking your mind. You may find yourself suppressing emotions or pretending to be something you're not, which leads to resentment, jealousy, and even feelings of inadequacy.

<u>Work in this section:</u> Uncover the patterns of negative speech that arise in your thoughts and words, including jealousy, criticism, and gossip. Ask yourself where these habits originate from and why you might feel the need to speak or think this way. Identify moments where you held back your authentic voice out of fear or judgment. This work helps you create space for your true self to speak freely and without the weight of toxicity. Through this process, you'll develop a healthier dialogue with yourself and others, and release the harmful behaviors that no longer serve you.

What does speaking your truth mean to you?
How frequently do you practice it?

Reflect on a time when you struggled to express yourself.
What held you back?

How do you handle difficult conversations? What strategies help you communicate more effectively?

Write about a situation where you felt misunderstood.
How did you respond?

Think about a situation where your boundaries were not respected. How can you strengthen your ability to set clear and firm boundaries in the future?

Reflect on your inner dialogue.
How do you talk to yourself?

What fears come up when you think about speaking in public or sharing your thoughts openly?

How do you ensure that you listen actively to others?

Reflect on a time when you communicated your boundaries effectively. How did this positively impact your relationship or experience?

Where in your life are you afraid to say "no"?
Explore how setting boundaries could create more space for your well-being.

Reflect on the ways you express love through words.
How could you enhance this?

How do you communicate your boundaries?
Is there room for improvement?

Write about a time when you felt heard and understood.
What made it possible?

How do you ensure your communication
is clear and effective?

What would your life look like if you communicated without fear? What changes would you make?

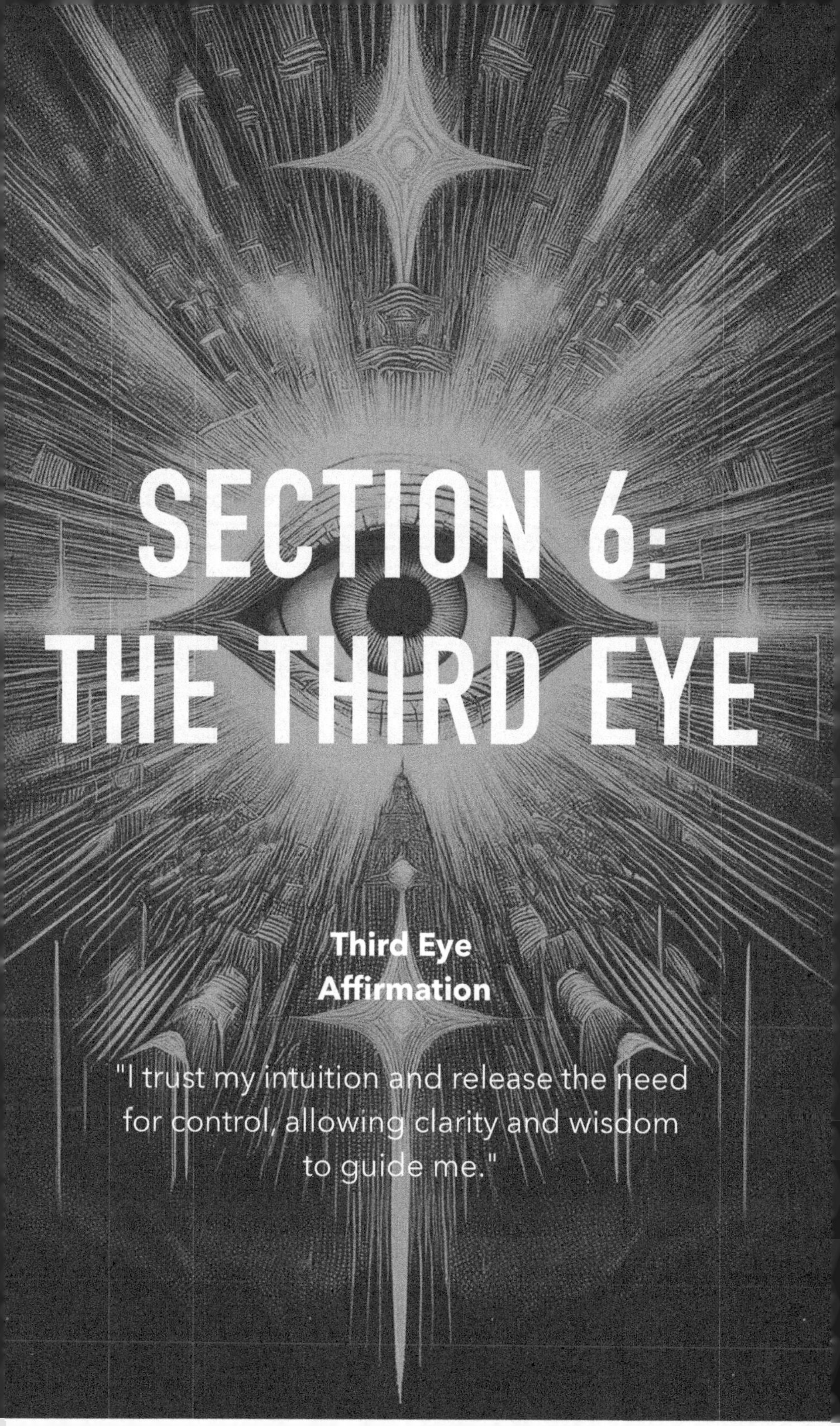

SECTION 6: THE THIRD EYE

Third Eye Affirmation

"I trust my intuition and release the need for control, allowing clarity and wisdom to guide me."

Section 6: The Third Eye

Focus: Intuition, Insight, Perception

This section focuses on dismantling blocks related to the third eye, which governs perception, intuition, and inner wisdom. A blocked third eye is often clouded by the ego or false self, manifesting as arrogance or a tendency to reject others' views in favor of your own. On the opposite end, it may show up as laziness or apathy, where your intuitive drive is stifled, leaving you stuck in a loop of inaction or avoidance.

Unchecked, these issues distort your perception of reality and prevent you from tapping into deeper truths. By working through these barriers, you'll reconnect with your inner vision and cultivate clarity.

Work in this section: Notice where the ego is blurring your perception, inflating or diminishing your sense of self, or preventing clarity. Use these exercises to help dissolve these blocks, allowing your intuition to flow and your insight to expand.

What does intuition mean to you?
How often do you trust it?

Reflect on a recent experience where ego or arrogance influenced your decisions. How can you cultivate more humility and self-awareness in similar moments?

In what situations do you find yourself acting from ego instead of intuition? How can you learn to trust your inner wisdom more deeply?

How does your attachment to being right or in control affect your relationships? Write about how letting go of ego could improve these dynamics

Reflect on a situation where your perception was clouded by judgment or bias. How can you work on expanding your perspective to see beyond your ego?

When have you ignored your intuition because of pride or fear of being wrong? Write about how you can better tune into your inner guidance and trust it over external validation.

How do you navigate situations where logic and intuition seem to conflict?

What beliefs or stories about yourself are rooted in ego? How might releasing these stories allow you to experience more clarity and alignment with your higher self?

Think about an argument or disagreement where ego took center stage. How could you approach a similar situation in the future from a place of empathy and understanding rather than defensiveness?

Reflect on a moment of clarity you experienced.
What led to it?

How do you stay open to new perspectives and insights?

What practices help you quiet your mind
and tune into your inner guidance?

Write about a time when you saw the truth
in a situation that others missed.

How do you balance rational thinking with intuitive insight?

What steps can you take to strengthen your connection with your intuition?

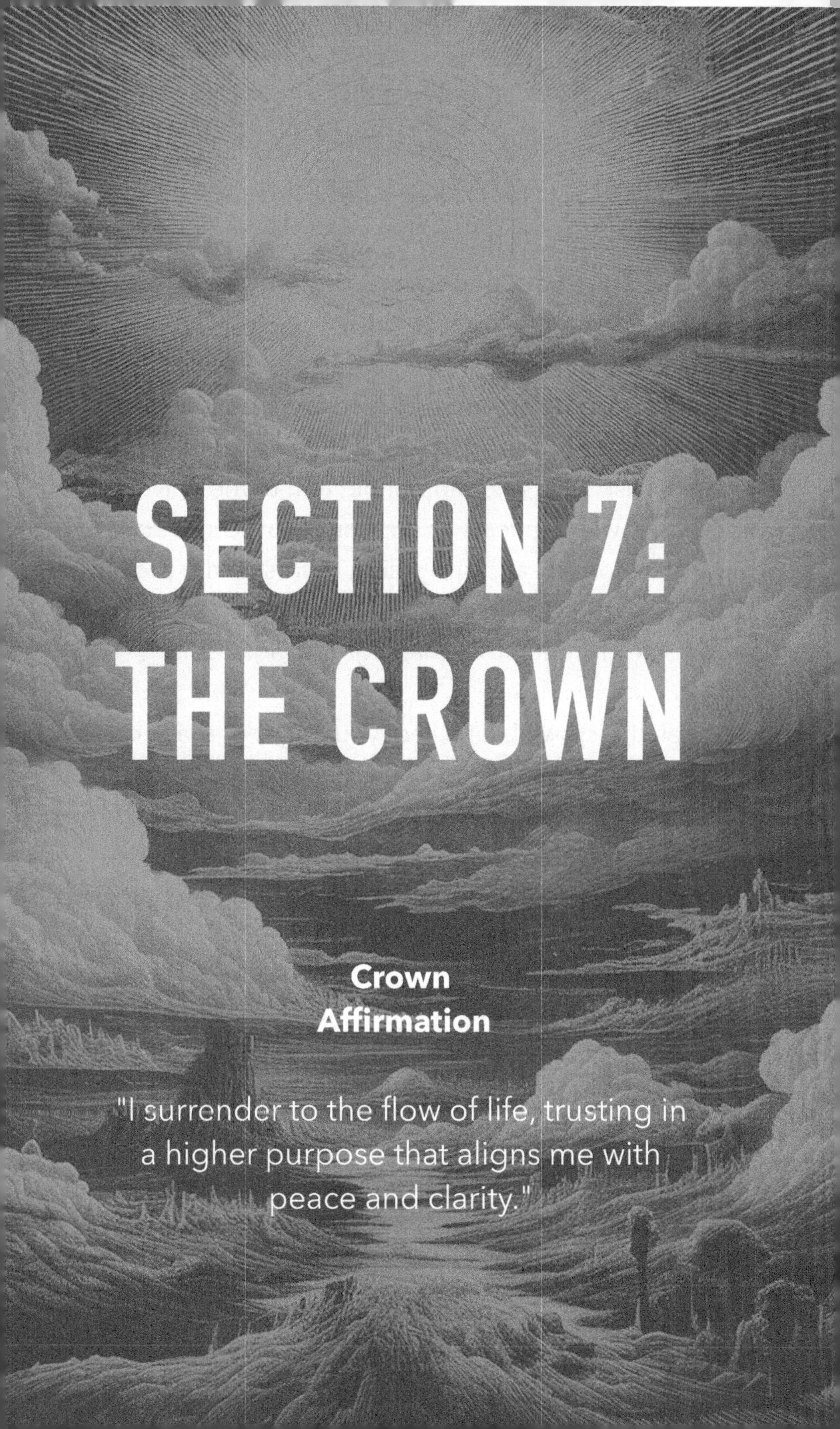

SECTION 7: THE CROWN

Crown Affirmation

"I surrender to the flow of life, trusting in a higher purpose that aligns me with peace and clarity."

Section 7: The Crown

Focus: Spiritual Connection, Higher Consciousness, Purpose, Surrender, Trust & Faith

This section is dedicated to dismantling blocks that hinder the flow of energy through the crown, which governs trust, faith, and our connection to the universe. A blocked crown manifests as resistance to life's direction, clinging to control, and struggling to trust in the process. Surrender and faith are crucial themes here – the ability to go with the current rather than fighting against it.

When the crown is blocked, you may feel a lack of trust in both yourself and the universe, leading to constant doubt, fear of the unknown, or feeling disconnected from a higher purpose. Opening this energy center involves relinquishing the need for control and allowing yourself to flow with the path unfolding in front of you.

<u>Work in this section:</u> Embrace surrender and non-resistance. Reflect on where you're paddling against the current instead of flowing with the direction life is taking you. Use the prompts to cultivate trust, strengthen your faith in the universe, and practice letting go of control. This process will help you align with a higher purpose, allowing peace and clarity to enter your life.

Write about a situation where you found it hard to release control. How would letting go have changed the outcome or your experience?

Reflect on a time when you felt connected to something greater than yourself. What was the experience like?

How do you define your life's purpose?
How closely are you living in alignment with it?

Write about a spiritual practice that brings you peace and clarity.

Where do you feel the most resistance to surrendering? Reflect on how releasing control in that area could open new possibilities for growth.

Reflect on what brings meaning to your life.
How can you incorporate more of this
into your daily routine?

How can you practice trust in the unknown? Identify one step you can take to embrace uncertainty and release the need to control every outcome.

Write about a time when you experienced a profound sense of unity or oneness.

How do you stay open to spiritual insights and guidance?

Reflect on your beliefs about the universe or a higher power. How have they evolved over time?

How do you integrate your spiritual beliefs into your daily life?

Write about a moment when you felt a deep sense of inner peace. What contributed to it?

How do you handle feelings of confusion or uncertainty about your life's direction?

Reflect on the role of gratitude in your spiritual practice.
How can you deepen this practice?

What steps can you take to align more fully with your higher purpose?

Notes Section:

Congratulations on taking the journey through the Unf*@k Your Energy Journal! The work you've done here is not just about healing or self-discovery; it's about reclaiming your power, aligning with your true self, and stepping into a life that reflects your highest potential.

Remember, this is a continuous process. The insights you've gained and the changes you've made are the foundation for ongoing growth. Whether you revisit the prompts regularly or explore new areas of self-reflection, the work is never truly finished.

Thank you for trusting yourself and this process. Here's to your journey of becoming the most authentic, unf*@ked version of you.

This is just the beginning! Continue your journey at goodstandard.co

GoodStandard

www.goodstandard.co

Made in the USA
Las Vegas, NV
11 October 2024

96692841R00134